Positive:

Get Out of The Hole of Negative Thinking

and Find Your Ultimate Potential

Valdemar Galvan

ISBN-13: 978-1470173067
ISBN-10: 1470173069

DEDICATION

This book is dedicated to my four little stars who were
my motivation to make things happen:
Kathy, Jimmy, Erick, and Isaac

CONTENTS

FOREWORD

Most of us live in a world where we let our lives run on autopilot, we assume that circumstances, situations, events, and experiences outside of us are what makes us, when in reality we can decide to take control of our own mind and life; we also speak a lot about self-worth without actually using it. Rarely do we come to the realization of who we really are and what our true potential can really look and feel like. If we became aware of the true nature of the excellence within ourselves, our lives would definitely become much more profitable and productive in all areas, not only would we be helping ourselves but we would be helping those that surround our daily lives, and with that, the world.

Our world always appears to be in a downward spiral with many bad things going on all the time, many people losing their jobs, many people not having enough to eat, people killing each other, many people finding themselves in deep depression, self-unworthiness, low self-esteem, failure, worry, fear, desperation, and anxiety. Our motivation grows thin, but as we put focus on these bad things, we essentially create more of those to see for ourselves and for others.

Having the desire to create positive change in your life is the first step into becoming aware of your true self. When you begin to learn and become aware of the knowledge of who you really are which by the way, has always been there yet most of us ignore; we rise up in believing in ourselves and begin to see no limits as far as what we can achieve. As we continue to accept, adopt, and pursue our personal growth, we begin to see the positive effects in our lives and start to see the world in a whole different way, and the world seems to respond, and reflect the way we see it as well.

INTRODUCTION

I'm about to reveal the lessons I learned and knowledge I acquired that started to change my life. Because you may be able to relate to some of the things I went through, I know that many of the things I will share here will help you as well in one way or another. I just want you to remember a couple of things.

Do not wait for others to change, do not wait for other people to make the changes that you believe will lead to the improvement of your life whatever difficulties you are going through, whether you are going through relationship challenges, financial, negative after negative experience, or not being able to realize your dreams or achieve success.

For things to change, YOU have to change your way of thinking, because you may not have control about outer circumstances and other people, but you can have control over yourself, and you can create your own reality whatever it is that you want, and however you decide it will look like. Remember this, no step by step program, book, or audio book into itself will really be able to change you. You have to want and desire the change before anything else.

Where it all begins is in changing the way you think, becoming aware of your own true self and realizing all the good and great things you have an immense potential for, we are all pretty much equipped with the things we need to better our lives in any area that we'd like to improve, this can be spiritually, financially, health-wise, our in our relationships. As you go through this material you will learn what I mean.

It is the intention of this book to spark an inspiration for you to start to realize who you really are, just as it started for me.

- Valdemar Galvan

1

About To Give Up

Because I focused on the negative things in my life, I only kept getting more of that on and on.

The day I decided I would no longer let negativity run my life is the day I began to see the light, it's like all of a sudden I had begun to let go of an old overwhelming weight I had in my back, and not only on my back but I felt it from my head to my feet, all the way to the inside of my being, and let me tell you it's not a good feeling. What kind of life is one where you work your butt day to day just basically to survive and the years go by without hardly any change at all! What kind of life is one where all you see are bad things going on everywhere you turn, how can you even find the motivation to change, how can you even begin to believe that you can actually improve your life when the world around you seems all messed up.

It is until recently that I came realize that it doesn't have to be this way. I made it that way because that's what I believed. I believed I was just meant to live this life of survival, which basically means just having enough to eat, a roof over my head and maybe the occasional treat, and believed this is the way most people and I myself were meant to live like, I felt it was something ongoing, including the way I was going to live until I grew old and died, and that it would never really change, after all, you get this idea from many people starting the moment you are born and throughout the years as you grow up.

Many people teach you to study hard and work very hard, teach you that life is difficult, teach you to play it safe otherwise you will encounter failure, and you develop the belief that you can't fail if you don't try, but that is where we miss out on life.

For many years I was trapped living in a life I believed was out of my control. It really began to hit me from the moment I became a young father. I remember myself in my last year of high school when shortly after I graduated I found out I was going to be a father. I really did have my struggles. I was 17 at the time I graduated and couldn't find a full time job; all places I ever applied were requiring me to be 18 to be able to offer me a full time position. But I was going to be a father and needed to work soon. I managed to find myself two part time jobs to support my new coming child, I had to ask for rides, take the bus and sometimes bike to work and even do some grocery shopping on my bike because I didn't have a car.

All this besides the fact that my dreams to go to college and get a career were practically crushed at the time, but it wasn't a priority anymore; I had bigger things now that I needed to worry about. After my child was born it went on pretty much the same, I lived in a one bedroom and almost crumbling apartment where our kitchen was no bigger than a small bathroom and could barely fit in a small round table with two chairs. As the years went by although I managed to get into a local vocational school, and get into online schooling which in turned helped out in going up career-wise everything else wasn't going so well at all.

I went through constant and ugly periods of financial stress, and even though I tried and tried to improve my knowledge in the field I was working at, thinking that this was the only way that was going to help me live and provide my family with a better life down the road, even though I kept slowly but steadily moving up in pay, It just never seemed to be enough. I always questioned and wondered where in the heck my money went.

As if this wasn't enough I went through various other difficulties, from relationship challenges, challenges involving my family and perhaps one of the biggest was due to the constant struggles and bad experiences by becoming stuck in deep negative thinking, even though I tried to remain optimistic at times and tried to be self-motivated, the negative circumstances outside of me always won. I came to fall in a deep level of depression and entered a period of self-sabotage beating myself up for being a failure because I felt that I tried really hard to succeed, and make everyone happy around me yet no one saw it! How could that be? In fact I was starting to be looked at as non-caring cold and robotic individual, even despite some of my attempts to change that. I became tired of trying and was about to give up.

I found out that I had been doing it all wrong I was constantly trying to make everyone around me happy and was trying to change other people's negative and pessimistic attitudes, the lesson there was some people simply do not have an interest in changing! The best you can do in that case is listen and empathize but know that you cannot change them, you may also wish them well and even send positive vibrations their way, as for people that are closer to you, give a little advice and positive influence but if you notice that they don't really take it seriously you then have to love them enough to allow them to find their own way. Sometimes it takes a good "shake" from life to wake us up and realize we want to change something that we don't like in our lives, that is just the natural way of how we learn but it is also the natural way we grow.

2

How My View Of Life Started To Change

Sometimes when you feel you are at the bottom and can't go down any further, the only option is to go up.

I found myself at "the bottom of the barrel" and really felt as if I really couldn't go down any further. Sometimes it takes a really bad experience that will get us to this point, and it is here where I believe many of us fall into drugs, violence, or addictions and other not so good escapes in an attempt to get away from what we went through. This is because once we are down this much we try to find things that will alleviate the pain of negative feelings, and we try to resist becoming vulnerable to anything related to the bad experience we went through. Although many try to find temporary relief in different ways, adding more negative alternatives is a sure path to self-destruction.

So there I was, at a deep down level. I only had two choices, to stay down there or rise up to the top. That's when it started to happen. Somehow from somewhere I found enough strength to really think about where I was and decided that I did not want to be down there anymore. Two words started to change everything for me from that point on, and those words were "positive thinking". Now this is how it happened. As I found just enough strength to want to do something about getting out of my negative situation, I went online and did a search on those two words, for one split second where I made the decision to get out of that hole I was in, I began to find resources that started to help me very slowly but surely and only grew and grew with time.

Soon enough one thing started to lead to another. I found references to great books and other material that I kept going after, and before I knew I had already gone through several books, audio material, and DVDs. I came across a documentary movie called "The Secret" where I was introduced to "The Law of Attraction". This movie made so much sense, and when I discovered that the inspiration for the movie was a book I had just read a couple months before, I became a great enthusiast. That book by the way is called "The Science of Getting Rich" which actually is not really about what most people think it's about as it hardly even mentions money as the main topic, but to learn more about you. This is one of the books that created an awareness that helped me change my life.

I started purchasing more and more material and I kept going through it with a very high degree of optimism and enthusiasm, it just felt good to begin to gain an awareness and knowledge that you just can't learn at school or any other typical educational institutions for that matter.

I discovered so many things. Some of those things are that you really become what you think fueled by what you feel and visualize. Another is that our beliefs are such a strong force that can really affect your life for the worse or good depending on what you choose to believe.

The fundamental part of really starting to learn about all this awareness starts with one thing however, and that is believing in yourself and learning how to master it. When you REALLY learn how to believe in yourself, the doors open up to endless possibilities ahead, and you become more confident. You start a journey of discovery where you learn all these different concepts in the world of self-improvement that you start putting together as in a puzzle and find out that with each piece, you become stronger and start seeing the world in a new and completely different way, a good way.

With that, I would like to say that investing in yourself and your personal improvement and development are the greatest investments you can ever make in your life, and there is nothing else that comes even close to it.

Remember for anything to change, YOU need to change.

"There is no greater sadness in death than that of one who passes without sharing to the world that which was special of him or her for the good of the world left behind"

3

How Can You Begin To Think More Positive?

Learning about the power of positive thinking can be the difference between being stuck in a hole and getting out of it.

We start to lose the ability to think positively as things go wrong for a long time. The best way to keep yourself thinking more positive is by associating yourself with positive things. Reading positive and motivational quotes helps tremendously because it stimulates your mind to think differently and more positively, and when you do it in a constant basis, it allows the reprogramming of your mental attitude. The main reason of why we think negative is because of an event or situation that has affected and stimulated a negative belief you had of yourself.

The first step to change persistent negative thinking, paranoia, or overreacting to small situations or experiences is to realize that these negative thoughts and the behavior that comes with them don't belong to our true self; it is only a negative personality.

Positive thinking is a mental attitude that admits into the mind thoughts, words and images that are conductive to growth, expansion and success. It is a mental attitude that expects good, favorable, and positive outcomes. A positive mind anticipates happiness, joy, health and a successful outcome of every situation and action. Whatever the mind expects, it finds.

Not everyone accepts or believes in positive thinking. Some see this subject as nonsense, and others just think of "weird" or even "crazy" of other people who believe in it and accept it. But even many of the people who accept it just don't know how to use it effectively to get results. Yet, it seems that many are becoming attracted to this subject, as evidence shows by the many books, lectures and courses about it. This is a subject that is gaining popularity with many bad things going around nowadays, people are looking for ways to improve themselves and seek ways to change their attitude and view of life as a whole.

You've probably felt down, worried, afraid, or depressed before and heard someone say to you "Think positive!" But the reality is that most people don't take this seriously, we hear it many times yet don't understand it, and people also don't take it serious because they may consider the term itself as not useful or effective. It goes in one ear and comes out the next in a split second.

What we need to do then is to actually study the subject to really grasp an understanding of it. When you do you will soon learn that many of the things you are going through in your life at the moment are directly or indirectly a result of your negative or positive thinking. If you really stop and think for a moment you will also realize how negative thinking really affects your life.

When we are going through our daily activities your positive or negative attitude strongly affects the outcome for the rest of the day. If you wake up with a negative attitude and negative thinking, you will notice that more and more bad things start to happen along the way. Say a person named Joe is getting ready for an interview in a new job, but Joe is one of the people who beat themselves up all the time, who has low self-esteem, considers himself a failure, or not being good enough.

Adding the fact that Joe has already applied at other jobs before without success, has now developed and gotten "proof" by not having gotten hired, that other people are better and more qualified. Filled with all these negative beliefs now "proven" into reality in the back of his mind, Joe gets up late for this next interview, and he finds out he has forgotten to iron his pants and shirt. Not only is he already running late but when he gets to the interview is full of fear and worry and is even sure he is going to be rejected, there is a strong lack of confidence and distraction. All this added up together not only did he leave a bad impression but he sure enough manifested this through his negativity and did NOT get the job.

Now let's look at the other side of the coin. Alex applied for the same job too, but his attitude was totally the opposite as of Joe's. Not only was he sure he was going to get the job but he had already been visualizing himself making a good impression, how they congratulated him for his new job and he also visualized himself as already working there. He prepared a day before and had everything ready, his pants and shirts all ironed and neat. The day of the interview he woke up earlier, had breakfast and took off early. When he got there, not only did he leave a good impression, but a few days later got a call offering him the job.

What you did not know is that Joe and Alex were both qualified for the same job!

Now, is there anything out of this world to this example? Nope. When we maintain a positive attitude, it then leads to pleasant feelings, constructive imagination, and within our mind start seeing what we would like to happen. If we put focus on examples like these, they start becoming more and more regular and not only do we start feeling happier overall but we also start manifesting more things to be happier about. We start to feel more powerful and confident, even our body language is affected. Everything in your life changes for the better.

I want you to remember something extremely important: Positive and negative thinking is contagious. However we feel whether negative or positive, in one way or another, we affect other people around us, and they get this at a subconscious level, through the way we feel and transfer those feelings, and through our body language.

There are many times when you can even feel or sense someone's negative or positive energy, you don't even need to know or physically see that they are behaving negatively. And what I meant earlier by subconscious level is that often times, that "negative energy" or whatever you want to call it, just gets to us through our thoughts and somehow start feeling it inside within our being. There is no surprise there then, why we don't want to be around people filled with negative energy AND we want to avoid it. People are more conditioned to want to help you also if you emit a positive kind of energy and dislike and avoid anyone emitting a negative kind.

We cannot change the way we think overnight, it is part of a process, but the very first thing we need to have is the desire to change it. After that, we need to begin to do work internally within ourselves first and train ourselves along. The power of our thoughts is a strong power that is always shaping our life, so start making those good thoughts if you really want to change it for the better.

We need to make a conscious decision that we want to change it. But listen to this; it is really at the subconscious level that we can make the changes permanent ones. You may decide to use your will to change your life for the better, your willpower is strong, but your willpower is part of your conscious level which means sooner or later it will fade away and won't be good enough. The way I see it is that 90% of you resides within your subconscious level and only 10% at your conscious level. Anything that you begin to store in your subconscious mind is what stays and what then turns to create the beliefs, habits and way of thinking.

Always try to visualize the good things. Use positive words in your inner self-talk and stop beating yourself up with negative words! Smile a little more; what you do with your body often affects the way you think, so smiling helps to stimulate thinking positively.

Try this just for kicks, stand tall and look with your head up and force a big huge smile while at the same time you try to think negative thoughts, you will find it is almost impossible to think negatively at that moment. Get rid of any feelings of laziness or desire to quit. If you persevere, you will transform the way your mind thinks. Ignore what others might say or think about you if they discover that you are changing the way you think, you will start to feel better about yourself, who cares what others think!

Once a negative thought enters your mind, be aware of it and take action to immediately replace it with a better serving thought. There are many things you can do to replace it, step out, listen to a nice piece of music, look at your baby's smile, and know what creates good feelings and head towards that. The key here is to be persistent, because with persistence you will allow and teach your mind to think positively and ignore negative thoughts.

Tips for thinking positively

1. Display a mental and emotional attitude that is positive to yourself and others.

2. Stay clear of negative internal self-talk.

3. Don't let downfalls; obstacles or difficulties impact your state of mind.

4. Do not allow what others say or think to affect your mind and spirits, remember that the true reality of how you feel comes from yourself and not what somebody else says or does.

5. Associate with individuals who bring positive things into your life and get away from those who don't plus kill your enthusiasm and optimism. Learn how to stay detached from them when you find yourself in their company and cannot avoid them.

6. You can spend great deals of time watching the news often times filled with garbage to your mind, meaning most of what they show is killings, devastation, and all the bad happening in the world. Be informed but not inundate yourself. Or you can spend that time improving yourself with self-help study material or other more productive activities.

7. Concentrate on speaking about the good things about yourself and others.

8. Research individuals who overcame hardships and are heading towards or found success in their lives.

9. Remember that whatever you expose your senses to such in what you feel, see, listen, and smell in a repetitive way, you will start programming in your subconscious mind, which in turn will have an effect in your life either positive or negative.

10. Place confidence in yourself and in your abilities

Positive thinking helps you cope with the challenges of everyday life. It brings enthusiasm, optimism, constructive thinking, inspiration, determination to look for solutions, and a whole bunch of other good things. It makes it easier to avoid worry and despair. Adopting it as a way of life will only bring you better things in all areas, and allow you with better opportunities for being happier and attain success. Positive thinking is a state of mind that is well worth the effort developing and strengthening by continuously striving to improve yourself.

4

Why Children Seem Happier Than Adults

There is more than the simple fact that most children don't have to worry about bills.

As we grow older we leave certain behaviors behind, sure we are glad there is no more bed-wetting but one of the best things we start leaving behind as well is our limitless imagination. Remember how a couple of blankets and pillows could transform the living room sofa into a magical fort? Or how a humble bathroom towel could turn an average boy into a superhero?

Children are happier because they look at the world with so much enthusiasm and excitement, you can hear a child describe and see the world as if they had no limits of any kind, and their imagination is wide open. It is until they start hearing feeling, seeing and learning about all the complaints from adults including parents, family and teachers that they start to experience a big bad world where dreams begin to fade, lack, failure and a number of negative things are also learned along the way. As we grow up we start seeing the world in a completely different way, and according to what we experience we start developing beliefs.

Unfortunately for the majority of us those beliefs are mostly negative. Beliefs that simply don't serve us well, beliefs that down the road only get bigger and bigger as we get stuck with them which by focusing on develop proof that in our minds render them as of being true. If we only kept some of the way we used to think as children we'd know that our imagination and self-belief could take us to almost unimaginable places and achievements.

It is never too late to go back to some of the characteristics we had when we were young. Use those in combination with the wisdom and experience you have acquired with age.

Play for example, has been consistently found to reduce stress, increases optimism, stimulates creativity, and increases your energy levels. So involve yourself with any activity that exercises the mind such as playing an instrument or any other activity of your liking.

Learning to think back like a child does, we start opening up the channel of possibilities that will allow us to believe in whatever we set our mind into by utilizing our imagination and see life with no limitations of any kind, always finding a way around.

"You can decide to think negative or you can decide to think positive, if you choose negative you will never get any positive results"

5

How You Also Help the World By Helping Yourself

The moment you decide to begin improving yourself you also help the world along with it.

You can have the most expensive personal development program out there but if the desire to improve yourself and the desire to change to a more positive you is not there it just won't work, you may learn a few things and hopefully it will inspire you to change and spark the motivation temporarily but if there is no true desire you won't get too far with it.

The good thing however, is that most people seeking personal development material will already have a desire to improve. It is really the first step into learning your true potential and becoming aware that you can create your own reality. But how can you help the world by helping yourself? You've seen great inventors of all time and great leaders, these people had an awareness that most lack and that awareness is learning your true power, there was a quote I read that said "You cannot help a man, you can only help him to find it within himself". All of us have exactly the same potential; we are just affected by our environment and learn to bury our potential with time by outer circumstances. Until you become aware and start believing in yourself, you come to learn that the only limits are those that are self-imposed.

When we start to master our mind and therefore our true self we can begin to help ourselves and all the people within your circle will be affected in a positive way by it, by you. It is only then that we go through our lives full of excitement and realization that we are capable to achieve whatever we set our minds into. It is through our momentum that we also affect the lives of others in and around the world.

When we find ourselves happy we then see the world in a completely different way, a good way, and those that are close to us will not help but to get some of that same energy we are emitting. You help the world by first helping yourself and once you're able to do that the world will notice and thank you for it.

6

Visualize To Manifest Things Into Reality

How the things we would like to have or achieve can be manifested through visualization.

When I was a young teen one of the first jobs I had was being a dishwasher at a local natural foods store part of my duties were to collect the garbage of all the offices in the building, I hated doing that and hated that some of the office people looked down to me and even treated me as if I was inferior to them. Sometimes I would visualize and imagine myself sitting in an office chair with nice soft cushion and armrests, sipping on a nice cup of hot coffee at the beginning of the day, not only was I taking my time to start the day but even imagined and saw myself doing a little chat with coworkers, I could hear the voices crystal clear, I could hear their smiles and good toned chat, and all that before beginning my day doing something I really enjoyed doing.

Wow, can you see how real I made it seem? Visualizing something so deep you even feel as if its real and there already, is such a powerful energy and only till you actually experience it yourself you will truly understand what I mean. By the way, yes I did actually make all that happen down the road oh and you can even add hot cocoa and tea. Visualizing and imagining can really take you anywhere you want as long as you do not let anything or anyone disrupt those feelings. Now go and ask yourself "what do I really want?"

There are however a few techniques you can do to help you come into this trance. Many self-help gurus recommend you to write your dreams or whatever is it that you want to achieve in paper, yes this does help! You see, the way I understand it and learned it is that by writing it down in present tense you begin to feel as if you have already achieved it, and the almost creepy part is when you start doing this and reading what you wrote every day you start experiencing opportunities, events, circumstances, people and things to make that happen! My own personal proof and simplest example is my website www.whatiamgoodfor.com that is how I actually created it and launched it after three years of procrastinating and thinking I wouldn't succeed, during those three years I dreamed a site to talk about positive things to help other people but I always turned myself off creating my own excuses that I didn't have time or there were other sites like that, hundreds of self-imposed roadblocks.

It is not until I actually wrote it down and read it constantly that one day I just went off started working on it and started writing some stuff...In about a week or less it was up live. Can you imagine after three years of self-imposed excuses and limiting beliefs I actually made it happen in a week! By the way from the moment I wrote my visualization down on paper and read it every day it took roughly two weeks when out of nowhere I started working on it. Now I want you to think about the potential of this in applying this simple technique with just about anything you want to achieve. If you align yourself with the vibration of positive thinking and self-improvement, in combination with this simple but powerful technique, the possibilities are endless.

"Being optimistic allows
you to see an opportunity
in everything, being
pessimistic does not"

7

Expressing Gratitude

When you express feelings of gratitude you start seeing and getting more reasons to be grateful for.

It is very important to have the feeling of being grateful of all the good things in your life. This feeling also goes hand in hand with the Law of Attraction. If we appreciate what we have, we send out positive "vibrations" that we have what we need to have in a present tense. There's a force out there whatever you want to call it but I seem to come across it being described as "universal force", anyways, this "universal" force will send you more of the same, and it will bring what you put your own energy to into reality.

The main thing is to reach a level of vibration where you begin to think very different from the rest of the world. By expressing feelings of gratitude you are adding more power to this state of vibration, it helps you remain in harmony with this state and you can even begin to see and experience more things to be grateful for.

Have you ever noticed that some people seem to complain just about any small thing that goes wrong, making a big deal out of it? Have you also noticed how these people always, always seem to have something wrong going on? What is happening here is that they are sending this kind of thought vibration into the universe and as a result keep getting more of that.

Expressing gratitude will work the same way except with the opposite effect.

Begin each night by expressing gratitude for the good things you experienced during the day and begin the next day in the morning by expressing gratitude for the good things you expect for the day.

Make a list of things that you feel appreciative of. You can start with by simply being grateful that you are well; have a roof over your head and food on the table. Spend time with your family and connect with the feelings of love and joy.

Help someone less fortunate than yourself. It can be a small act of kindness but doing this can make you feel good about yourself and realize how lucky you are in the position to be of help.

It doesn't matter what you do have. Just be thankful for it! Even if all you have is the shirt on your back, or tore up shoes, hey, be grateful for it. You will experience a great feeling each time you express gratitude, but the best part is that this creates an energy that will create more things for you to feel more grateful for, just learn to pay attention because as you do this you will experience more opportunities that you may not notice otherwise.

8

Your Feelings Are Trying To Tell You Something

Pay more attention to the way you feel at any given moment, our body and mind are amazing in many ways and this is just one of them.

You've probably noticed on your car that as it finds something wrong such as low on oil or maybe it displays a warning sign in the form of a light with a symbol that appears, it basically telling you there is something wrong or is giving up a warning that if you don't change the amount of gas and put some more soon it will leave you stranded somewhere in the middle of nowhere, OK maybe not to that extreme but don't put gas and you run the risk of getting stranded soon.

Our feelings are an example of this, they tell you when something is not right or on the other end too, they tell you when something is good. You start feeling sad or mad or lonely, hungry, emotionally hurt, resented and it's your inner being telling you something is not right, but keep paying closer attention to your feelings and if for example you find out that you are feeling stressed constantly or everyday then right there is an obvious flag that something is wrong and you need to take action to change it and change it fast! Our feelings are a way to let us know whether we are going in the right direction or not.

On the other hand, If you associate with good positive people, activities, and other things that make you have positive feelings, then you are going in the right direction.

This concept is so powerful that it is even scientifically proven that if you are feeling bad or stressed your body is in risk of being affected by it in a physical form. Even in sickness you may have found out yourself that feeling good and positive allows you to heal faster if you have really paid attention. Our feelings in combination with what we believe are so powerful in ways we don't even fully understand yet.

"You can let your mind sink you in a deep hole, or you can take control and allow it to help you prosper"

9

What Is Reality?

Everyone has their own definition of reality but did you know you can control your own one to how and what you want it to look like?

You may think that the life you live day by day is real, after all why would you think otherwise if what you live day by day is what you see, what you hear, feel, smell, and taste. But is it? Your neighbor next door or your friend's cousin may completely disagree with what you say is real because their life may be completely different from yours, they don't experience the same things you do, so can't we say that their view of what is real is also what is real aside from what you think is real?

Each and every one of us has our own concept and definition of reality. If your life is full of problems, misery, and almost all of it full of negative stuff going around it then what your concept of what is real is most likely that life just sucks! And all you strive to do is merely survive it day to day. But let's say we ask a person who has wealth, health, no stress, and is just happy overall, well I can tell you that with certainty that person will tell you that life's reality is great! Can you see the picture here?

We have to realize that we were all built with the same potential for great things whether we currently see it or not, and need to realize and become aware that we can shape our own reality, and it begins with a single decision based on how we answer but one question.

Albert Einstein once commented "that the most fundamental question we can ever ask ourselves is whether or not the universe we live in is friendly or hostile" and hypothesized that your answer to that question would determine your destiny. We have but one general decision to make on how we want to live our life. And because you see it a certain way doesn't mean that this is reality, it's your own current reality! As a matter of fact there is not even such thing as reality because reality is a term that we all define individually the way you see it based on what you've experienced and from those experiences you developed beliefs which in turn make up your individual concept of reality.

You can change and re-program your current reality, because what you are currently living is a result of your past experiences, behaviors, and way of thinking which in turn created a program with certain beliefs. When you have had negative experiences in the past and have developed bad behaviors, you have created a "program" or belief that the reality of life is a bad one, and this then becomes the way you live your life, focusing more on the bad experiences or negative things in life.

Remember how I constantly listened to personal development audios and read all these books on personal development? I immediately started to turn my life around into a new positive awareness because I was doing it so much and so often that I started to "reprogram" my mind without even knowing. You see, doing something in a repetitive basis, creates a program in your mind, this program develops habits and in turn creates your beliefs and concept of reality.

If you want to reprogram your mind from whatever your current beliefs are at the moment, whether you believe you are not good enough, you are not happy, you don't want to try something because you know you will fail, or you are too afraid of taking certain actions that you know will potentially lead to a better life, then you must not only fill your mind with good stuff but also do it in a repetitive way. Get personal development books, audios, DVDs, etc. and listen or read often, do it every day! After around a month you will start to see the world in a different way, you may even start to notice better things happening around you, simply pay attention.

10

The Law Of Attraction

You attract what you think and focus on most, whether you choose the negative or positive things, that is what you will attract more of into your life...it always works this way.

You know it's just amazing how things work sometimes. For a long time I had been using this so called "law of attraction" in my jobs and later on career-wise, and I knew there were higher forces at work but just didn't know what to call it or how to describe it, all I would do is visualize and believe and doing that created some really nice things for me by allowing me to advance from a job to a career. I utilized many of the techniques that come with it even though I did not know then that they were part of this law. "Techniques" sounds way too inferior though, as it's really more like a type of set of "energies" that we are barely beginning to tap into as human beings.

Now this may not be making much sense to you yet. So let me give you a crash course into it. I believe strongly in this law because when I started learning about it thanks to a great personal development and self-help guru named Bob Proctor it just made total sense to me as many of its descriptions were things I had been using previously in my jobs before I even came to learn about it. It is important to mention that one major thing I realized was that we can use this law for just about all areas of our life not just in our job or career! This is the part I was missing as I was doing fine growing and going up career-wise but other areas in my life where not so great and in those areas I seemed to focus more on the negatives and kept getting more of that as well!

I have read and heard many explanations from people out there who understand this law yet it seems it is sometimes easier to understand it within yourself once you understand it rather than explain to someone else. So let me tell you what the law of attraction is as I understand it. There are laws in the universe, such as the law of gravity, there are energies or forces out there that exist yet we can't necessarily see. The law of attraction is one of them and it states that we attract what we think about most, and attract what we put our energy and focus on most. The law of attraction basically works through what we think about consciously but given power to from our feelings and from there on creating a subconscious awareness that creates some kind of invisible "universal energy" which then in turn makes circumstances, events, and situations happen that lead to us obtaining and attracting that what we think and focus on and what we want. The law of attraction is not biased however, and if you think, focus, feel and put energy into negative things, negative things you will also attract.

I have become fascinated with all studies related to our human potential and mind and let me tell you, everything seems to have some kind of connection. I have learned that we are equipped already with most of the things we need to succeed in all areas of our life but we become our own roadblocks, and close ourselves to great and good limitless possibilities out there.

If you want to learn more about the law of attraction and go beyond, learn about The 11 Forgotten Laws at www.selfhelpgurusnow.com

"The adversities and struggles we have in life are the ones that truly make you grow, if there were none there would be no growth and therefore no point in life"

11

Appropriate Rest Is Essential

Inadequate rest will not only halt any progress when setting up goals and wanting to achieve them but it may also initiate procrastination.

I cannot stress how important it is to get appropriate sleep and rest well. This is actually one of my greatest challenges because time it seems is scarce when you are trying to study something or do anything for that matter when you have a family and/or a job and a thousand other things that you need to attend and take care of. I used to have this really bad habit of sleeping very late (OK at the time of this writing I still do but I will be working on it) I'm talking about 2 or even 3am, because I had created the habit and belief that this was the only time I could do anything else I wanted to do such as writing the material for my website or this book. I come home around 6pm from my day job and well it seems as time just flies from there on till it is time to go to bed.

What I found out is that this negative habit of sleeping very late at night, when I had to wake up around 8am actually became counter intuitive and I discovered I actually ended up losing more time this way, and that was because the next day my level of energy was just so low that so many days I felt exhausted by mid-day and all I thought of doing was just going to bed right after I go off work, this also affected other things such as my health, I was feeling tired all the time, I had no energy left to attend my family and often times this resulted in attracting more negative situations as many of these times I felt in sort of a bad mood being easily bothered by noises from the T.V. and kids playing around.

One of the other bad things about this habit was that I actually had no energy to do the things that started to change my inner self, I had no energy therefore didn't feel like reading any books or listening or watching any videos or any of that, all I kept thinking was in landing on a soft comfy bed or couch and just passing out. For so long I've done this until recently it started to change for the better I started looking into Neuro Linguistic Programming and self-hypnosis audios, it was something new to try but I didn't mind giving it a shot. Found out many of these techniques work very well and you should definitely look into them as well.

12

The Importance Of Setting Goals

You really have no direction in life without setting yourself goals. It's like walking in a dark room with no lights on.

Goals are a very important aspect of our life. We are rationally thinking creatures; we don't live by instinct. That is the reason we need goals that can help us take from one point to another in our lives. Going through our lives without goals is like sailing without a compass; uncertain of the direction we are going whatsoever. When we are at school, our goals could be to achieve a particular grade; when we are in college, our goal might be to score a particular mark to get admission in a certain professional course; when we are able to work; our goal could be to get hired in a particular company or organization and so on. If you think about it for a moment, we are always setting goals for ourselves and trying to reach them, the key is to actually write them down to help us get focus of them, otherwise we may forget what it is we are trying to achieve and can lose motivation and focus.

If you aren't establishing goals already, you are leading an unplanned life; you are going through it with no direction. Now let me ask you something, do you want to live? Or do you want to exist? Because if you don't set goals in your life you aren't living; you are merely existing! You are merely taking life as it comes.

However, a person who has goals in life has one very important benefit. They come to know what they are really worth. If you have set a particular goal for yourself and you achieve it, you know you are capable of that. This makes you gain confidence in yourself. You know now that this was something you could do and you achieved it. This is not just something on your resume; it is something that is now recorded in your life – it has become a part of yourself. And it will reinforce the belief you have in yourself.

For example, say you set a goal to earn a hundred thousand dollars in the first six months of your business. When you are setting that goal, you are only shooting in the dark, whatever the factors that influence your goal-setting might be. But then you really achieve this goal. Now, you know that wasn't shooting in the dark. You know you are capable of such a thing. It has made you believe in yourself and you can go and plan bigger things.

The way I learned to set my own goals was like this: I break down my goals into smaller chunks. It's almost like taking on a huge chore. For example, say you are in need to clean your whole house, just by thinking about it will squeeze the heck out of your energy and you will start "lazying" out, it will seem that it will take you forever to finish, so that will most likely kill it and you will end up putting it off for who knows how long. But if you decide to break everything down further, then it becomes more achievable. You divide the concept of cleaning the whole house and break it all into smaller chunks, such as cleaning the kitchen, the yard, the room, the bathroom. Reduce that even further, to cleaning the refrigerator, or taking the garbage out. By breaking your goals into smaller sections they start looking and becoming easier to achieve. Take my example of how I personally set my goals:

- Year goal
- 3 month goal
- Monthly goal
- Weekly goal
- Daily goal

Starting with setting yourself goals even small ones to begin with will pave the way to achieving an increasing amount of goals and allow you to attain what you used to think as of hard to achieve things. Suddenly the impossible becomes possible and your mind starts to expand with an almost unlimited belief of the things you can achieve.

This is what goal-setting does. They solidify something that's just a hazy picture, or a vague idea. Goal achievement makes you realize your strengths and helps your self-belief in an enormous way.

"You can't truly help others unless you help yourself first, when you help yourself you are also helping others"

13

The Importance Of Helping Others

Inspire cooperation by helping others and they will also help you.

Thousands of people can be walking on top of a goldmine and never realize it. If you but learned to "wake up" and become aware, you would then use your imagination to dig down into the earth and discover the riches down there. The riches found within your own self.

In order to not just walk over it but to actually find it, we need to investigate and use our imagination. We are stuck with life as we know it and tend to do the same things every day. We are routine creatures. There is really no way of making new discoveries without getting out of our comfort zone or our routine, we need to get out there, get curious about ourselves and other things, read the book, watch a totally different type of TV show, do completely different things, meet new people and new places.

If you are young, then you should consider yourself very fortunate to start learning this early in life. You can develop, extend, and always add to your curiosity and imagination. Wherever you are, whoever you are, and whatever you do for a living, there is always room to make yourself more useful and more productive by developing yourself.

All of our growth and achievement in life comes down to each of our individual efforts to begin, but you cannot completely succeed without the co-operation of other people. I have come to the realization that we are all here for each other, without each other we are nothing. There would really be no point in life to be here just for ourselves and by ourselves.

But before you can arouse cooperation from other people to help you succeed, before you can have the right to expect or ask for help and cooperation from others you must first be willing to help them. Always be willing to do more for others, yet never forget and abandon yourself either, just remember that by cooperation with others you can draw on infinite intelligence that can help everyone involved succeed.

14

The Power Of Enthusiasm

Enthusiasm affects others as much as it affects you; make use of this extraordinary power.

By being enthusiastic we stimulate the mind and inspire ourselves to take action. Enthusiasm is contagious and affects not only the person feeling it but it also affects the ones around us. This feeling will allow you to go through just about anything and make it seem almost effortless, it energizes your body so much that even when you are feeling lazy, or even fatigued a sudden burst of enthusiasm will give you a great boost of energy throughout your body.

To give you an example of the power of enthusiasm let's say you love music and you also like to dance, in fact, you have a few kids, the husband or wife doesn't like going out much or have had so much work or any number of tasks that have kept you busy and haven't had a chance to go have fun dancing in a while. As a matter of fact you haven't had any kind of fun in a while at all.

Have you ever noticed how sometimes you come home from a hectic day at work all tired and don't feel like doing anything else? Say your cousin comes to visit you, and you're lying in the couch yawning, tired and frustrated beating the darn remote control to try to make it work knowing the batteries are already dead. Your cousin says "hey, I noticed you haven't gone out in a while and x band is coming later tonight and the admission is free, I already talked to my mother and she will watch the kids, do you want to go?"

Suddenly you jump up in one split second full of excitement thinking hey I haven't gone out in a while, that sounds great! SO you talk to the husband, wife or friend and they agree to go with you, in fact they too get a little excited themselves. You begin to think to yourself, wow this is good. Suddenly you start making plans on what you will wear and stuff, you realize you need to run to get some quick groceries to the store and leave some snacks for the kids or plan to give a couple other friends a call to invite them. Where did your lack of energy go! It's gone! All of a sudden you have completely forgotten you were even tired and are now full of energy and ready to have some well-deserved fun that you haven't had in a while.

Apply this to any kind of feeling to your work or activity that you do and you will see it makes things a lot easier. Both, it energizes you, and at the same time spreads that energy to people around you in a good positive way.

Some people are naturally enthusiastic, but others must learn it and acquire it. One way for you to acquire it if you don't have it is to do things you like and enjoy doing. If you are in a job where you really don't like much of what you do, focus only on something you do like about it, this will help you survive until you find a better opportunity or start slowly building it and developing to the point of having built enough to move on to better things.

Enthusiasm is not something spoken about that only exists in thin air; it is a force that you can take advantage of, learn to harness and use. Without it you would be no different than one of the dead batteries on that remote I mentioned earlier.

"*Whatever you put in your mind will reflect your results through your thinking*"

15

See Your Failures As Learning Opportunities

There is no such thing as failure, only feedback. When you start seeing failures as learning opportunities, you can create situations that otherwise would not be there.

Most people believe failure to be something bad, demeaning, and negative by nature. For many people failure has led to a significant number of not very good endings and grief, it is sad to see that many have even taken their own lives by dwelling too deep in that sentiment and state of mind.

In reality failure is more something temporary rather than putting the meaning of "end" to it. It really doesn't end here unless you believe to see it that way. Failure is obviously not a good feeling at all nor a blessing, although when you learn to develop your self-awareness you can even begin to see it that way, you can to a certain extent; begin to see some of the beauty in failure. Once you do start thinking this way you will be able to redirect your energy along different and better ways. You will learn to create opportunities from failure.

The way we grow in life is by NOT putting resistance to the adversities and bad experiences we go through in life. When we put such resistance to these events including failure; we become stuck, if it's bad experiences we've had with others this resistance usually evolves into resentment, with failure it starts to turn into self-sabotage eventually and potentially leading to a deep state of depression.

I myself have gone through many different kinds of failures. But taking a look at them from this point, before I really started to change my way of thinking, now I know that what looked to be a failure was nothing more than a kind, unseen form of help, that stopped me in whatever I was doing at the time and with great wisdom forced me to change my efforts and ways along to more better and rewarding roads.

Somewhere along the road as part of my readings I came across a nice little true anecdote. There was this guy, let's call him Tony. Tony had gotten a new car, so just like any other day he parked his car and went to work, now the only difference he did this particular day was that he failed to park correctly and parked too far away from the curve but didn't think it was a big deal. After some chatting with coworkers he decided to invite them for lunch. As he came out and glanced towards his car he noticed a huge dent in it, some distracted soul had just ran into it denting side of the fender and scraping a good portion of paint. Now most of us would probably feel like getting a hold of that person's neck and twisting it good. Sure it wasn't a good feeling at all, and he wasn't covered insurance-wise either. Sure enough Tony wasn't happy and excited about it.

But instead of focusing too much on the anger and discomfort, Tony decided to somehow turn his failure of not having parked right into something positive by creating an opportunity from it. He went to get estimates for his car repairs and found out it would cost him $800 to repair. He didn't know quite how but he said to himself and intended that he would do a business deal or something to double that amount within 60 days. About a month later still having this intention in his mind he created a business deal that not only doubled but quadrupled the amount equal to his repair costs. All of a sudden not only had he covered the costs but also made three times that for himself!

Just imagine this, what are the chances that if this hadn't happened to him he would have created this intention? Sure he might have still created some kind of deal, but it sure wouldn't have contained the same amount of power as his intention gave him.

This previous example is just a simple way of how we can decide to take our failures and turn them into opportunities that otherwise would not be there. All we have to do is open our mind to creating these opportunities and combining them with a real intention that is followed by taking action.

As I came into one of the greatest turning points of my life I realized that those failures were necessary for me to advance developing myself and keep growing making me realize that there are good and bad things in life, but whatever we choose to see and believe in more starts to change your inner self and later as your growth starts to reflect not only on the mere outside of you but can even reach and span at great amount of lengths and horizons full of capabilities and opportunities.

Can you imagine a world without failures? There would really be no growth because it is due to these that we truly learn what it is to be human.

I have felt thankful in a way for having had sense enough to realize that strength and growth come only through continuous effort and struggle. Each temporary defeat allows you to appreciate future successes and add more value to them.

16

The Power Of Your Mind

When you begin to learn about the capabilities of your mind, you come to realize that you can achieve just about anything you set your mind into.

A very famous personality in the field of personal growth and self-help by the name of Napoleon Hill said "Whatever the mind can conceive and believe, the mind can achieve regardless of how many times you may have failed in the past". With that simple but true statement, the possibility of using one's mind to overcome obstacles, problems and mistakes, and the attainment of success and achievement is projected.

Sometimes, mind power is also loosely described in the form of affirmations. Many believe that affirmations can help lift damaged spirits. If you don't know what an affirmation is, like I did before my way of thinking started to change, an affirmation is you being in conscious control of your thoughts. They are short, powerful statements. When you say them or think them or even hear them, they become the thoughts that create your reality. Affirmations, then, are your conscious thoughts. An affirmation into itself is not really what starts to create your reality but what it does by programming those thoughts in your mind until your subconscious finally accepts it. I don't believe that any scientifically designed drug or medication works as effectively as mind power.

In some cases, using the power of the mind to control an outcome or break a negative trend can be life changing too. For instance, if someone has been going through a cycle of bad relationships, there is a way of breaking that chain and prevent history from repeating itself. If you look into self-hypnosis, for one thing is also a way to control the mind and help your own mind control your actions.

When you start tapping into your mind, you really begin to tap into your inner powers, and remember that if you learn how to control your own mind, you can tap into limitless opportunities and unleash a powerful version of you that can achieve the most out of life. It's true. The subconscious mind can be controlled and can be used to your advantage.

Let me just point out for clarity's sake that the brain and mind are for most people, the same thing. I see as brain being a more physical term to describe the organ within our body that does the thinking, and mind as a more spiritual word not tied to physical boundaries. For many successful people and those who understand and comprehend the power of mind control know that the brain and mind are therefore totally different things.

You use the brain to make decisions when there's been a mistake, or when doing analytical or logical thinking. But you don't use the mind for that. You use the mind to connect the feelings, including your love, interests, passion, and beliefs.

I cannot begin to illustrate or describe that knowing and learning how to use the mind is extremely empowering, and you will notice the difference the moment you start to tap into it.

Successful people are success-minded, and that is what makes the difference from those who make it and don't. When you are success-minded, you will spend time every day mentally going into yourself, evaluating your own needs, requirement, goals, mistakes, where you put your focus on, and talents. This process of going into yourself is a key concept of having mind power potential.

We all value and want different things, but let me ask you, do you want that nice house you saw last week, or that new car model you saw at the dealership a week before that? Go then and ask your mind for one.

When you start tapping into the power of your mind, and start raising awareness of its potential, your potential, YOU can overcome anything, even financial burden. You always find a way to go around anything to get to what you want, if you really plant it in your head it almost becomes automatic to the point that you even start becoming aware of opportunities that come your way that get you a step closer to attain what you want. If you really want it, your mind will help you create a plan to achieve it.

> *"If you but decide to*
> *believe you can attain it*
> *you will"*

17

Success Is One Of The Greatest Motivators

Keep success alive by keeping your motivation alive as well.

When we want something and are fascinated by it, it motivates us to act with the goal to attain it. Let wanting to live in a bigger house or have a better job that will give you a bigger paycheck be your motivator. Why not? We know that the biggest challenge to succeed at what we want is lack of motivation. But sometimes we get discouraged halfway and drop everything, and often times have a million starts towards achieving what we want but not see the end result.

Don't lose sight of success then. The fastest way is to keep your eye on it all the time on a constant basis. Do not get distracted by obstacles and roadblocks, always focus on the day you're going to get whatever is it that you want, how does it look like? What does it feel like? Can you hear any sounds associated with it? Dwell upon those senses and learn to see all these things that you could be missing out on if you decide to give up. When you see success as not an option but a fact, the faster you will make it happen.

I'm not trying to demean or offend anyone but hanging out with the wrong people can have a dramatic impact to your success, so what do you do? Start surrounding yourself with success-minded people. Start following, studying and figuring out what they did and are doing, and if you have the opportunity to ask questions ask! Many successful people will be happy to answer your questions because many are actually glad that there are people who look up to them and admire them. When you surround yourself with people living in success, you cannot ignore it. This plays a very important part of keeping your motivation going.

So surround yourself with successful or success-minded people and you will reap the rewards. Not only will you be able to keep your motivation up but there will be a time where you can start a relationship and find yourself in a position to motivate each other and share some tips and tricks. You could be the greatest positive and optimistic person in the world but you will still be susceptible to feeling negative, sad, disappointed, impatient, or worried about achieving your goals. Positive and success-minded people can sympathize, understand you, and even offer a shoulder to cry on and then help you by giving you a little push back up.

One thing I had seen time after time as I started getting into the study of self-development and personal growth is the creation of what many call a "vision board". Create a vision board, you can even do this as your computers desktop image by cutting out pictures of people or things that remind you of your goals and let yourself dwell on the success every time you go through it. If you can associate yourself with the success or goal you would like to attain in as many senses as possible, the more power you create to turn it into a reality or the faster you will manifest it.

18

Who Am I?

Am I really a piece of meat with bones running around like crazy?

As I continued to study more into the self-improvement material, I started noticing that although some of the teachings of many well-known self-improvement gurus out there varied somewhat, there was one thing that I noticed they coincided in. This one thing really started to catch my attention and am to the point where it all starts to make sense. It is also why I don't even remember seeing the word "money" in the book "The Science of Getting Rich" when I at first expected this book to be a complete how to get rich via the means of money and stuff type of guide, to my surprise I learned money is just a tool and where we really begin to be rich is within ourselves, everything else just evolves and develops from there on.

That one thing is that we are not really this physical body with meat and bones running around, nor the name we have, nor the things we have.

We are way more than that! Somewhere along my studies I remember studying about this scientist specializing in quantum physics describing how we thought as matter or the smallest possible unit of what all things are made of to be "physical" but in easy to understand words my understanding is that there is no physical at the smallest level, there is just empty space or "energy" hence we are not something physical at our core.

If you've seen the way a magnet works, that to me seems like a good example of this, the magnet is attracted to metal instantly, put two magnets against each other and you feel the magnetic energy field repelling one another, you can't see it, yet you know it's there!

We are something like that energy field, at our core we are more of some sort of energy, the only difference is that we are conscious of ourselves unlike anything else in nature.

This is the essence and key of where our true potential and power originates from. If we but only knew how to "feed it" continuously we'd grow with such an awareness that would truly allow us to see no limits ahead.

The good news for you is that all of the content on this book will help you by attaining the essential knowledge to "feed" our conscious energy and the way to feed it is with good positive things and positive thoughts. Learning to be aware and take control of your mind and continuously striving to develop this idea is a key.

> *"A man is but the product of his thoughts what he thinks, he becomes"*
>
> *-Mahatma Gandhi*

Conclusion

You have now learned some of the best things I started to become aware about that helped me change my way of thinking and my view of the world in general. Before reading this book, you probably only had a distorted and ambiguous view of yourself or the way you looked at people and things around you. Many of the difficulties and challenges I went through were ones that not only brought me down but had I not made the decision to change it; this book would have not existed with the potential of helping you and others.

My hope is that some if not all of this material has helped you in one way or another and inspired you to take action in changing the way you think, because most of us think in a negative way, and it is this what limits ourselves and holds us back from achieving big and great things and the way we live life surrounded by family and friends.

Learning to become aware of whom we really are and our own potential not only helps us in one but all areas of our lives. Becoming inspired is the first step, followed by the desire to take action. I would like to encourage you to follow me through my website and through my emails as I will continuously share the things I learn with you. Join me in this journey of self-discovery as I am determined to help you in any way I can. I know that helping each other we can achieve big and great things in life.

About The Author

Valdemar Galvan lives in California. He is passionate about personal growth in general, and is fascinated with the human mind and our human potential. It is how he got started into creating a vision and goal of helping others while at the same time striving to continue to improve in all areas of his life, he is a strong believer in the Law of Attraction and studies various other subjects such as Neurolinguistic Programming, Hypnosis, EFT, and other related self-help material. Val is also passionate about web and computer technology. Enjoys reading and writing, spending time with his family, and is always looking to expand his knowledge and awareness to share his learnings with other people all over the world.

Follow Me on Facebook for Daily Inspiration
www.facebook.com/HowToThinkPositive

or Twitter
https://twitter.com/Think2Positive

Find out more about me at:
www.WhatIAmGoodFor.com

Quotes

"There is no greater sadness in death than that of one who passes without sharing to the world that which was special of him or her for the good of the world left behind"

"You can decide to think negative or you can decide to think positive, if you choose negative you will never get any positive results"

"Being optimistic allows you to see an opportunity in everything, being pessimistic does not"

"You can let your mind sink you in a deep hole, or you can take control and allow it to help you prosper"

"The adversities and struggles we have in life are the ones that truly make you grow, if there were none there would be no growth and therefore no point in life"

"You can't truly help others unless you help yourself first, when you help yourself you are also helping others"

"Whatever you put in your mind will reflect your results through your thinking"

"If you but decide to believe you can attain it you will"

73

"A man is but the product of his thoughts what he thinks, he becomes."

-Mahatma Gandhi